I0006327

JAVASCRIPT - THE FIRST STEPS

DAVID HOCKLEY

KODAPS ACADEMY

CONTENTS

CHAPTER 1
PRESENTATIONS AND PREREQUISITES

H i! My name is David, and I've been working in Game and Web development for over 2 decades. And I love coding. I actually started coding when I was about 8. I did so on a computer called the ZX81 released in 1981. It had less computing power than most basic watches have today.

And code is my passion. I love building stuff in code, and understanding how to make code work. And I love helping people understand how it works. I hope to help you discover what makes code so fun and exiting. I'll be explaining the basics of how JavaScript works. Of how to code in JavaScript. I'll be using practical examples that you can follow along with on your computer. Now who is this for?

Well, are you fascinated by coding, and you want to understand how code works but don't know where to start? This course is for you. It uses JavaScript, the most common programming language. It teaches the basics of code. What variables and expressions and operators and control flow are. So that you can better understand what code is all about.

Do you already have the basics of HTML and CSS, and you want to become a full-fledged front-end developer? This course is also for you. We'll be covering everything you need to know to get started. We'll be building a solid base for you to build on.

Have you already started dabbling in JavaScript, by copy-pasting examples? And are you missing the theory behind the practice, which is holding you back from shining. This course is also for you.

Whatever stage you are at, my goal is to help you reach a point where you are self-sufficient. Where you can not only copy and paste and adapt code, but write your code from scratch.

A point where you're able to start using a front end framework such as React. (And if you don't know what that is, don't worry: we'll get to that in due time). I aim to provide a solid foundation of both theory and practice.

I've always learnt by doing. So, this course will be providing you with many opportunities to try things out by yourself. You'll find resources accompanying the different chapters. Now, we'll be taking the time to explain everything, but we'll be looking at some fun concepts along the way.

An important question, before we go any further : why JavaScript? And what is TypeScript? What is the difference between TypeScript and JavaScript?

As I've said, JavaScript is the most common programming language there is. Every single browser runs it. It can also run in many other places. For example, it's one of the more popular choices for server languages.

In the StackOverflow developper survey, the language developers use the most is JavaScript. 2/3rds of the respondents said they use it. And moreover, 30% said they use TypeScript, which is JavaScript with superpowers. And 34% said they use NodeJS, which is JavaScript for servers.

So, JavaScript and its variants are the 1st, 6th and 7th most used languages among all developers. And 1st, 5th, and 6th among professional developers. This means, JavaScript is a critical tool to have in your toolbox.

As an added bonus, it also has quite a bit in common with other languages. Its syntax was inspired by a language called "C". (You may have heard of its more modern counterparts, like C + + and C#). It can be a stepping stone towards those languages. Or indeed towards other languages that share the same parentage, such as PHP.

All these reasons combine to make JavaScript (and TypeScript) great languages to learn. And you've come to the right place to do so!

There are one or two things you need, however.

The first, of course, is access to a computer you can install stuff on, and in the next chapters we'll be looking at useful tools. Now, before we go any further, let's take a look at this simple JavaScript program, run within a web page.

Take a look at it, and try to imagine what it might do :

———

```javascript
// this is a comment,
  // it is ignored by the program
  const you = "World";
  function hi (name) {
    return 'Hello ' + name;
  }
  const message = hi(you);
  console.log('message:', message);
  const appDiv = document.getElementById('app');
  appDiv.innerHTML = `<h1>${message}</h1>`;
```

———

Don't worry if you don't understand every detail (or even if you don't understand any of it). We'll be going through it all in detail. What I suggest you do now, however, is to take the time to play around with this code to try to understand what it does.

If you go to https://kodaps.dev/js-sandbox you'll find a sandbox with this code, so you can experiment to your heart's content. We'll be using this sandbox to build up an interactive webpage as a class project.

This sandbox uses a tool called StackBlitz. This allows us to edit and run JavaScript within the browser, without installing anything.

As you can see in the central pane, there is the code. On the left there are the files, currently we're editing a file called "index.js". And on the right there is the output.

That output, the part on the right, is actually separated into two panes. This is because there are two different types of output.

Now feel free to play around with this code, and see what changes in which output.

For example, you could try changing the value of name, and set it to your name. Or you can try changing the behaviour of other bits of code.

Please don't hesitate to start experimenting. You can't break anything, and if it stops working, just reload it from the link and start again.

And when you're done, we can move on to the next chapter!

And to recap: In this lesson, we've gone through all the reasons why JavaScript is a great language to learn!

CHAPTER 2

THE VITAL TOOLS — CHROME DEVELOPER TOOLS, NODE JS & TYPESCRIPT

N ow, before we get started, there are some essential tools that we need before we start coding in JavaScript...

Well, that's not quite true. We'd be able to get along with only the playground and a text editor. But you're on your way to becoming a fully fledged developper, so let's get you the tools you need to get where you're heading!

CHROME

The first thing you will need — but that you probably already have — is a browser. That being said, Chrome is by far the most used. So if you don't have that, it might be worth installing it: it contains several tools that are very useful for developers. In fact, if you don't have it, install it now. I'm going to walk you through some very useful tools it provides.

Once Chrome is started, click on the three dots to the top right of the screen, and then down to "more tools".

This opens a sub menu, and in this sub menu we find several entries. The one we're looking for is "Developper tools".

When you click on developper tools, it opens a new pane on the side.

This pane has various elements and tabs.

First, we have the "inspector" cursor and the "screen device" toggle. These are vital when coding in HTML, but less so when we are focused on JavaScript.

This being said we will be using the inspector at times, it works as follows : first select the tool, then click on an element on the page. The **Elements** tab will open up, and show the HTML that produced the element you just clicked on.

And since we're going to be listing the tabs, the Element tabs shows all the HTML on the page; you can fold and unfold and even edit HTML elements. You can also see the JavaScript code when it is directly on the page and not pulled in from an external source.

Cool, huh :)

Next we have the **Console** tab. This is going to come in *very* handy because JavaScript code can write messages here. It is also where errors show up, so I usually have the console open when I'm developing. Let's open it up.

On the side, at least in Chrome, there is a pane that allows you to select the level of error message that you want to show. There are different levels of severity. There are crashes and errors, there are warnings, and there are informational messages. You can click on the first item to see them all, or on each level of severity to only see the messages you're interested in.

Let's go ahead and click inside the console pane.

You can actually type code here. For example, let's type console.error("There is no problem")and press enter.

As you can see, this prints out a red error message saying there is no problem.

We can also type "console.log("Hi")" and a "Hi" message will show up.

These two tabs are the most important ones for us.

The other tabs are:

- The **Recorder** tab that allows you to track performance issues across several pages. We'll steer clear of those for now. This is currently a preview feature, so it might change.
- The **Sources** tab that allows you to see all the places the page is getting its data and code from.

- The **Network** tab shows network messages that occur once it has been opened, so if we reload the page, we can see the timeline of network messages and data the code is sending back and forth. If we click on one of the messages, we can see some of the data that was exchanged with the server. We'll use this when we start looking at how we can use JavaScript to talk to an API.
- Finally, we have the **Performance**, **Memory**, **Application**, **Security**, and **Lighthouse** tabs that allow developers to make sure their webpages are working well. They're very useful, but are outside our scope for now.

So as you can see, there are already a *lot* of tools inside Chrome, although we'll mainly be focusing on the inspector and the console.

NODEJS

Now that we've had a look at Chrome, where your code will be executed, let's take a look at a tool that was born from Chrome.

Because the JavaScript engine was packaged into a standalone program so that it could be run on servers.

That standalone program is NodeJS. And this program also allows us to run JavaScript code on our computers without having to run a browser each time.

So, let's head over to nodejs.org and install NodeJS!

This will also install another tool, called NPM, that allows developers to install libraries and tools.

If you click on the terminal, you can check that NodeJS is correctly installed by typing "node -v". This will show the current version of Node that is installed.

You should also be able to type "npm -v" and this should also show a number.

Now that we've done that ... we're ready to move on to the next vital tool!

CHAPTER 3

THE VITAL TOOLS – THE IDE (EDITOR)

N ow the next tool you need is an "IDE" or integrated development environment. To be honest, code is just text files, so any pure text editor can produce valid HTML and JavaScript code. You might like to try out Sublime Text or Atom.

That being said, there is one tool that is used by most developers. That tool is called "Visual Studio Code". And like Chrome, it is free. Its main advantage is that it supports a high number of languages via extensions.

Now, unless you're very lucky, you probably don't have Visual Studio Code installed yet. To install it, you just need to head over to https://code.visualstudio.com/ and follow the instructions there.

There is even a pure web version that you can use if you go to https://vscode.dev/. However, it is not a final stable version and has certain limitations, so I will be using the installed version.

Now, I've installed various extensions via the extension marketplace. If you click on marketplace and then type "theme" in the search bar, you'll find many themes displayed. The one I use is called "Luvia". There are other nice ones to try out, I like One Dark Pro too.

Now, most extensions are actually useful, not just colourful. I recommend you get two for now:

- Prettier, which will help make sure your code is properly indented and
- ESLint, which will help find mistakes in your code

Now that we've played around with extensions and customised our tool, let's get actually using the editor!

Click on "file" then "Open folder" and click on "EmptyFolder". The tool will ask you if you trust the authors of this folder. You can either click yes or create a different empty folder!

Now, in the pane on the right, we can right-click (on Mac use Control click) and select "New file".

Let's call it "index.js", and just type "console.log("Hello");"

Now if we click "Run" in the top menu we should have an entry that says "start debugging", and it should offer several versions. If you've followed along, you should have NodeJS as an option.

Click on that, and you should have a new pane open up, and if you click on "Debug Console" you should have the "Hello" message show up.

And with that, we should be good to go!

CHAPTER 4

HELLO, YOU!

L et's start getting introduced to JavaScript, and playing around with our little program and understanding what everything done. Here it is again:

```
// this is a comment,
// it is ignored by the program
const you = "World";
function hi (name) {
  return 'Hello ' + name;
}
const message = hi(you);
console.log('message:', message);
const appDiv = document.getElementById('app');
appDiv.innerHTML = `<h1>${message}</h1>`;
```

MEET THE CONSOLE

There is an unwritten rule of any language that you have to start by learning how to say hello (or more precisely: "Hello World") with your code.

And as you will probably have guessed, that is what the code above does.

(Link: https://kodaps.dev/js-sandbox)

However, it does so in two different ways.

On the right of our screen, if we follow the link, we have two panes. Both show the same message :« Hello World ».

What are these panes?

Well, the top pane is the visible output of our code, and the bottom pane is what is called the "console".

Did you know your browser also has a console? How to access it depends on each browser, and the language it is in.

In Chrome, for example, we click on the three little dots under the profile, then "more tools", and then developper tools. The exact method depends on each browser, but I've listed them all in the workbook.

And to write to the console, we wrote the following:

```
console.log('message:', message);
```

Let's try changing that around for now, and just writing

```
console.log('Hey folks');
```

As you can see, "Hey folks" now appears in the console. Now, let's try something else, and type the following

```
console.log(you);
```

Notice there are no quotes around you. Can you guess what will show up?

The correct answer is … "world". Why is that? Let's take a look at the code again.

At first, we have

```
const you = "world";
```

This line is defining a value for a *variable* called you. What is a variable? One way of thinking about it is a box that can hold a value. One single value. As you can see, the youdoesn't have any quotes around it. When we ask it what it contains, it tells us. So, when we call :

```
console.log(you);
```

That is just as if we had written

```
console.log("world");
```

The box's content is sent to the console log thingy. Let's try something a little different. What happens if we write:

```
const you = "world";
const message = "hello " + you;
```

```
console.log(message);
```
What do you think the result will be?

If we look at the line
```
const message = "hello " + you;
```
Here, too, the "you" variable provides its value. We mash the word "hello" and the contents of the variable "you" together, and we put it in a new "box", a new variable, called message.(Incidentally, that mashing together is what we would call "concatenation".)

And, so far, we've only been assigning variables, we haven't been changing the variables once they've been assigned. That's why we declared them using the const keyword, which stands for "constant". (So basically we've been creating variables that don't actually vary.)

If we wanted to change the variable later, we could have used the let keyword, like this:
```
let age = 12;
age = age + 1;
console.log(age);
// note : the above prints 13
```
You can also see that we can use a variable on both sides of the =assignment operator. On the right side of the =we read the value of age (12) and add 1 to it. Then, on the left side, we assign the new total (increased by 1) back to the sameage variable.

We couldn't have done that if we'd used the constkeyword.

A "keyword" in this context means a word that has a reserved meaning. A keyword can't be used for anything other than to mean that reserved meaning.

An example of a keyword that almost anyone who has come in contact with code knows, is "if". We'll be taking a look at how that work pretty soon.

But when we say that keywords are words that we can't use, that means there are words that we can use. But where could we be able to use them?

The main place is actually… variable names.

VARIABLE NAMES : RULES AND RECOMMANDATIONS

What are variable names?

For the moment, we've used names like "you" and "message", but we could have used "me" and "greeting" instead and the code would have worked the same. What we can't do is to give the variable a name like "const" or "if" because those are reserved keywords. There are a few other rules you need to keep in mind reading variable names, and some recommendations.

The **first** is that they **must** be a single word (or blob) of text, that is to say, they can't have any spaces in the middle. So welcome message is not a valid variable name, JavaScript considers that to be two bits of code. But welcomemessage is fine, although difficult to read. However, we'll see how to improve on it shortly!

The **second** thing to note, is that variable names can start only with a letter or an underscore. They can't start with a number, for example. So 1directionis not a valid variable name.

(A quick note: Technically variable names can also start with a dollar sign, but developers seldom use dollar signs in variable names except for some very specific cases that are way beyond our scope here).

The **third** rule for variable names is that they can contain letters (both upper and lower case), and numbers, and underscores.

And bear in mind that variable names are case-sensitive. This means that messageis not the same as MESSAGEwhich is also not the same as Message

We can't use welcome message (with a space in the middle). But because we have capital letters and underscores, we can actually call our variables something like welcomeMessageor welcome_message. That first way of combining words is called "Camel Case" (or "camel-Case") because the words have bumps in them, like camels. The second way of combining words with underscores is called "Snake Case" (or snake_case) because it hugs the ground like a snake.

These are both valid ways of doing things, in terms of what the language allows, but for variable names within JavaScript I'd recommend using camelCase. As you might have noticed, we start out with a lower case letter in our variable name. This is not a requirement of JavaScript, it's just a naming convention that developers use.

And we use it because it allows to start variable names with an upper case letter when it is something more important (like a component in a framework, or a class).

A FEW LAST WORDS ON VARIABLE NAMES, AND READABILITY

If you've been following along, you'll have understood that x123and thisIsAVariable are both valid names.

However, just because you *can* do this doesn't mean you *should*. There is a saying, that code you've written more than 6 months ago might as well have been written by someone else. And one way to help your future self (or another developper) understand your code, is to use variable names that are as readable as possible and help understand what is going on.

So for example, if we were trying to calculate the distance between two arbitrary cities, we could use city1Position and city2Positionand distanceBetweenCities

There's no real limit on the length of a variable name, but if it is too long, it stops being readable! What you can do is try to play around with the variable names in the playground.

One thing you should be aware of, though, is that when you change a variable's name, you need to alter it everywhere it is used.

So if you change this:

```
const you = "world";
console.log(you);
```

to this:

```
const hello = "world";
console.log(you);
```

You'll end up with an "undefined" because you is no longer defined.

Your turn now, try defining new variables and seeing what you can do with them. Using the let keyword, try to create variables and then change their values.

Exercice 4.1 : As a final exercice, let's say we have a and b that are variables that have been defined at some point, e.g.,

```
let a = "value b";
let b = "value a";
```

We've seen how to reassign values to variables (by using = without the letkeyword), how would you ago about (without editing those initial lines, which are just an exemple) swapping the two values contained by "a" and "b"? You're up!

And just to recap : In this lesson, we've talked about :

- using the console
- creating variables with the letand constkeywords
- what keywords are
- how you can and should name variables

CHAPTER 5
SMOOTH OPERATORS, IS IT TRUE? (CONDITIONS, TYPES, OPERATORS AND FALSY VALUES)

Now that we've started using variables, and putting values into them, it's time to move a step forwards. We're going to be looking at conditions, and control flow. Do you remember our age variable from the last chapter? Let's pick up from where we left off.

———

(Exercise 5.1)
```
let age = 10;
if (age < 18) {
  console.log('A life of coding awaits');
} else {
  console.log('Time to party (and to code)!');
}
if (age >= 65) {
  console.log('Age is in the mind, really.');
}
```

———

Here, we've started using a staple of programming: conditions. Try to guess what happens when this code is run? What do you think is printed out?

Now, what if we were to change the value of age to 42. What would happen then? What about if age were worth 81? Take the time to try it out and see what happens.

Now, before we have a look at how if behaves, let's take a closer look at age < 18 and age >= 65.

These are examples of "expressions". Let's try to explore this a bit more. What do you think the code below will show?

_____

(Exercice 5.2)
```
let age = 10;
console.log(age < 18);
console.log(age >= 65);
let overTen = age > 10;
console.log(overTen);
```

_____

Here, age is a variable that we set to 10, and overTen is a variable where we store the value of the expression age > 10.

These expressions evaluate to either true or false. This is what is called a boolean. Here age < 18evaluated to true, and both age >= 65and overTenare false (age is equal to 10, so it is not strictly superior to 10).

That means we've now seen three types of values that can be stored in a variable : strings (i.e., text), numbers and booleans. Now, back to our if statements. The way if works is, theif has a condition, and two curly brackets ({ }) that define a block of code. And *if* the condition is true, then the code inside the block is executed.

If the if also has an elsestatement, then if the condition is true, the first block is executed, otherwise (i.e., "else"), the second block that comes after the else is executed.

WHAT IS A CONDITION?

We've seen one or two in the examples above, but for now, I'd like to look at one of the most basic conditions. Equality.

Is this equal to that?

And JavaScript actually has two different equality operators. And right now, you're probably wondering what on operator is, and why JavaScript has two just for equality. We've seen what variables and values are. Well, an operator is something you use with values and variables. So, for example, + is an operator.

(And by the way, age + 1 is an *expression* : It's a combination of values and variables and operators that produces a value. In the same way age > 10is also an expression, it produces a boolean value, i.e., trueor false.).

We've already used one operator quite a bit : the assignment operator. When we write let age = 42 the =sign here is the assignment operator. And while we're looking at what things are called, : let age = 42is called a statement. It does things but doesn't "produce" a value. The if construction is also a statement. So, an expression is a bit of code that produces a value, a statement just does something.

Anyway, back to our equality operators. Like I said just before, there are two of them : == and ===. Now, I'd like to be able to tell you to just use the triple equality operator (===) and not the double equality operator (==). And as a rule, you should really only use the triple operator.

But in practice, once you start coding you are bound to come across code where the double operator is used, so we need to explore the differences between these two.

———

A lot of the time, both operators work the same.

```
let foo = 42;
console.log(foo == 42); // true
console.log(foo === 42); // true
```

· · ·

```
console.log(foo == 43); // false
  console.log(foo === 43); // false
```

————

Here, both of the expressions (foo == 42and foo === 42) evaluate to true. Now, at this point you're probably wondering what the difference between these two operators are, and rightly so. The triple operators check whether two values are exactly the same, so it corresponds to what we'd expect from an equality operator.

The double operator checks whether, values are the same once they've been convert to different types.

So for example "0" === 0 is false because one of the values is a string and the other is a number, so they are not exactly the same number. But "0" == 0 is true because if you convert that first "0"to a number, then it would produce 0.

Now, that example looks fairly straightforwards. However, what happens if we look at "" == 0 ? Well, when JS converts the empty string ""to a number, it produces 0. Therefore, "" == 0is true.

JavaScript considers that 0 and "" are "kind of equal", and so zero and the empty string are "double equal", or to put things differently, (0 == "") is true. This means that we can easily imagine a situation where we have three variables, let's call them a, b and c.

And these three variables are such that "a" double equals "b", "b" double equals "c", but "a" does not double equal "c". (Or to use the technical term, double equals is not "transitive"). How do we achieve this?

```
let a = "0";
let b = 0;
let c = "";
```

```
console.log(a == b); // true via type conversion
  console.log(b == c); // true - both are falsy
    console.log(a   ==   c);   //   false,   no   type
conversion
```

Here a and c are not equal : they are both strings, there is no type conversion to carry out, they are simply not the same value.

On the other hand, both a and b on the one hand, and b and c on the other, are "kind of" equal. The triple operator doesn't have this problem, since none of a, b, or c are triple equal to anything apart from themselves.

In other words, a == b and b == c, but we don't have a == c. In code terms, a !== c. Or: "a" is not double equal to "c". Which is the opportunity to introduce three new operators : !, !== and !===.

Now, ! means "not".

So !true is false. And both !== and !=== function as the negation of their counterparts without the not sign in front, so "" !== "0" for example, and 0 !=== "0".

Before we move on, can you guess what the following code produces?

```javascript
if (0) {
    console.log("Zero");
}


if (!0) {
    console.log("Not zero");
}
```

JavaScript considers some values to be "kind of false", on falsy to use the technical term. They're not strictly the same as false, the boolean value. But they are values that, when put in an if statement, will fail that statement.

These values include 0 and "" but also concepts we will be seeing shortly like null, undefined and some that are outside our current scope and that we won't be talking about for the moment, namely : Nanand 0n (the BigInt representation of 0). Conversely, any value that is not "falsy" is "truthy".

So, this means that the code inside the brackets will not be called:

```
if (0) {
  console.log('this will not be called');
}
```

```
if ("") {
    console.log('neither will this');
  }
```

However, the code inside these brackets will be called:

```
if (42) {
  console.log('this will be called');
}
```

```
if ("the meaning of life") {
    console.log('as will this');
  }
```

Exercise:

A value stored is stored in a variable (a). We want to transform it and store the result in a new variable b. We want b to be true if a is "truthy" and false if a is "falsy".

There are two ways of doing this : using if and else or using the !operator (several times).

```
let a = someValue;
// what 1/ construction with "if" or 2/
expression
// can we use so that b is false if a is falsy
// and true if a is truthy ?
```

```
let b;
```

To sum things up, in this chapter we've seen :

- The if and if ... else statements
- Boolean types (true and false)
- The not (!) operator
- The double and triple equal operators (== and ===), and their negated equivalents (!== and !===)

CHAPTER 6
LET'S GET LOOPY!

We've seen equality operators and conditions, now is the time to take a look at a staple of programming : the loop.

For this, we're going to calculate the value of a factorial. Now, a factorial is a mathematical notion mainly used to calculate probabilities, and it uses the "!" notation, although it is placed after the number. It's fairly simple to understand, let's start out with a few examples :

$3! = 1 \times 2 \times 3$,

$5! = 1 \times 2 \times 3 \times 4 \times 5$

That is to say : the factorial of a number (let's call it n) is the product (the multiplication) of all the numbers up to that. So n! is "$1 \times 2 \times 3 \times 4....$" and so on, all the way up to n. There are several ways of calculating this, one of which is just to use the factorial operator (!), but the goal here is to use a loop. Let's calculate 10! and then we can go over the code together :

```
const n = 10;
  let factorial = 1;


for (let i = 2; i <= n; i++) {
```

```
    factorial = factorial * i;
}
```

```
console.log(factorial);
```

You should end up with 3 628 800 — factorials climb fast.

The first two lines should not be a problem. The interesting "bit" is the forstatement. As you can see, the part that follows it (in between brackets) has three parts to it, separated by semicolons. These three parts are what define the loop. Now before we look into them, let's talk about what comes just after: we have curly brackets (and these define a block, remember). Inside that block, we update the factorialvariable by multiplying it with the value in the ivariable. What is iworth ?

Well, that is precisely what the fordeclaration is ... for.

Let's look at the three parts :

- First : let i = 2: this is the initialisation. It sets the initial value of ito 2.
- Second : i <= n: this is the **end condition**.
- Third : i++. This is a new notation. It could have been written i += 1or i = i + 1. All of these three do the same thing, they increment the i variable by 1.

What does fordo ?

First, it runs the initialisation (here, it sets ito 2).

Then it checks the condition. If the condition is trueor even just "truthy", theforstatement runs the block, that is to say the code between the curly brackets.

So, the first time, iis worth 2, so when the block runs the first time, factorialis multiplied by 2. Once the block runs, the forstatement executes the third statement. Here, that statement increments iby 1, so now iis worth 3.

As 3 is indeed smaller than n (since n is worth 10), forruns the block again, so now factorial is worth "1 × 2 × 3" (i.e., 6), and increments i again, which is now worth 4. This continues until i is worth 9. The forstatement runs the block, then increments iwhich is now worth 10. As 10 <= 10, the block runs one last time with ìset to 10.

And then the loop increments i, and as 11 is bigger than 10, the block of code is no longer run, and factorialis now worth 1 × 2 × 3 × 4 × 5 × 6 × 7 × 8 × 9 × 10, i.e., 3 628 800.

Now that we've seen a simple example of how forworks, let's take a look at one or two things that are worth knowing. First, the third statement in the loop doesn't have to increment the variable by one. For example, if we want to count down from ten, we could do :

```
for (let i = 10; i > 0; i = i - 1) {
    console.log(i);
}
```

Here the loop starts out at 10, prints that out in the console, then removes one, and prints the result, and so on until iis worth 1, and is printed out. In the same way, if you wish to print all the even numbers between 1 and 100 you could do :

```
for (let i = 0; i < 100; i += 2) {
    console.log(i);
}
```

There are two more things to see. First, there is another type of loop called while. The idea is to simple repeat the same block of code, as long as the condition defined is valid.

```
while(condition) {
    // do this
}
```

For example, our loop calculating the factorial of 10 could be written as :

```
const n = 10;
let i = 2;
let factorial = 1;


while( i <= n) {
    factorial = factorial * i;
    i++;
```

```
}
```

The forloop and the whileloop can both do the same things, I would tend to use the forloop when I know where my loop stands and ends, and use whilewhen I am looking to fulfil a condition but don't know exactly when it will happen :

```
while (youDontSucceed) {
  pickYourselfUpAndTryAgain();
}
```

A typical use case for this, and the opportunity to introduce the third important keyword of this lesson, is when we want to have an infinite loop that we break out manually. If we write :

```
while (true) {
  ///
}
```

This loop will go on forever. Thankfully, there is a keyword that allows us to break out of a foror a whileloop. That keyword is break

So, our factorial could also be written :

```
const n = 10;
let i = 2;
let factorial = 1;
while (true) {
  factorial = factorial * i;
  if (i > n) {
    break;
  }
  i += 1; // or i = i + 1; or i++; they all
mean the same thing
}
```

Here, the whilekeeps looping indefinitely, and it is the breakwhich allows us to stop the loop when the right conditions are met. To sum this up, in this lesson we've seen:

- the "for" loop
- break

- while
- the ++operator and the +=operator

As a final exercise, there is a code test that is sometimes used in coding interviews. It's called the FizzBuzz test.

The idea behind the test is, for all the numbers between 1 and 100 :

- if the number is a multiple of 3, print Fizz
- if the number is a multiple 5, print Buzz
- if the number is divisible by 3 and 5, print FizzBuzz
- and if none of those conditions are met, print the number itself.

The output should look like :

1, 2, Fizz, 4, Buzz, Fizz, 7, 8, Fizz, Buzz

Now is probably a good time to introduce the %(or rather, modulo) operator. This tells you what the remainder of a division is. So, 7 % 3 = 1 because 7 is 3 × 2 + 1. Or when you divide 7 by 3 you get 2 with a remainder of 1.

This means that "x is a multiple of y" is the same as "x modulo y equals 0". There, you should have all you need, have fun, and please don't hesitate to reach out if you're having trouble.

CHAPTER 7
FUN WITH FUNCTIONS

FUNCTIONS 101

We've seen different types of values that we could put into variables : number, string, boolean. It's now time to see a new type of value.

Let's have a look at the following code. Can you guess what it does?

```
function add(a,b) {
  return a + b;
}
```

```
console.log(add(3,5));
  console.log(typeof add);
```

In this code, we've created a new persistent variable and given it a value. Can you guess where it is?

The second console.logshould give you a clue : The variable we've created is add, and it is a function.

As you remember, a variable is something you put things in. This variable actually contains reusable code, functionality that you can call on. And the value it returns is determined by the returnkeyword.

To call that code, we "invoke" the function, and to do that we add parentheses after it with the values we want to use in the execution. So in our example above, the add(3,5)means "execute add, with a set to 3 and b set to 5". As it is a variable, we can assign the value to other variables.

```
function add(a,b) {
  return a + b;
}
```

```
let plus = add,
```

```
console.log(plus(3,5)); // 8
  console.log(typeof plus); // function
```

Do you remember the loop where we calculated the factorial value for 10? We can now put that in a function, and calculate the value for any value we can't, without duplicating the code:

```
function factorial(n) {
  let f = 1;
  for (let i = 2; i <= n; i++) {
    f = f * i;
  }
  return f;
}
```

```
console.log(factorial(3)) // 6
  console.log(factorial(5)) // 120
```

Instead of re-writing the loop so each different value we want to calculate the factorial of, we can just call the function. This allows our code to be "DRY" which is important. Here, DRY stands for: Don't Repeat Yourself.

As you've probably guessed by now, console.logthat we've been using quite a bit is also a function.

You will most likely come across a different way to declare functions, using the "fat arrow" notation. So in our add example above, we could actually have written :

```
const add = (a, b) => {
  return a + b;
};
```

The "fat arrow" part is the equals & inferior (=>) part. It's worth noting that in this case, where a function only contains one return statement, it can be written on one line :

```
const add = (a,b) => a + b;
```

Now there are some differences between the fat arrow syntax and the normal declaration, but they are way outside our scope, so we won't be going in to them.

Coming back to the factorial function, a small detail which has its importance. It's worth noting, we can actually call the function within the function itself.

Now since n! = n x (n - 1)! (you can think it through or take my word for it, the point of this is not to go into the maths), we can actually write the factorial function like this :

```
function factorial(n) {
    if (n > 1) {
      return n * factorial(n - 1);
    } else {
      return 1;
    }
}
```

The returnstatement breaks the flow of the code : once we reach a returnstatement, we leave the function. Therefore, we don't need the elsestatement, we can just write the above function like this :

```
function factorial(n) {
    if (n > 1) {
      return n * factorial(n - 1);
    }
```

```
    return 1;
}
```

DEFAULT PARAMETERS

In all our examples, we've always specified the parameters of the function when we've called it.

However, it's possible to specify default parameters. For example, we could have the following function :

```
function incr(nb, step = 1) {
    return nb + step;
}
```

Here, is step is not specified, it will be worth 1. It's not the most exciting function in the world, but it allows us to do the following :

```
let nb = 1;
nb = incr(nb); // only increase by 1
nb = incr(nb, 2); // increase by 2 this time
```

An important point to note : you can't have parameters *without* a default parameter *after* parameters with default parameters.

Which makes sense, since JavaScript wouldn't know which parameter is being defined!

CALLBACKS

As I mentioned above, functions are variables. Now we can't really add them together, but we can use them as parameters when we call other functions.

So, for example, we could have:

```
function completed() {
    console.log("All done");
}
```

```
function work(done) {
    // doSomeWork();
    done();
```

```
  }
```

```
work(completed);
```
Here completed gets sent to the workfunction, under the name done, and the workfunction calls donewhich prints out "All done". What is the point of this?

Let's say we have behaviour that takes a bit of time. For example, we're talking to a server, or we've set a timer. And we want to instruct the code that "when you've finished, (for example when the timer runs out, or when the server responds), then do this new thing". To take a closer look at that, we're going to look at timers.

TIMER

The "wait a certain time" function already exists. It's called setTimeout, and it takes two arguments : a callback function, and a delay measured in milliseconds. (And for your information, you need a 1 000 milliseconds to make one second). Let's try using it together. Let's take a look at the following code :

```
console.log("pre");
```

```
let done = () => console.log("done");
```

```
setTimeout(done, 1000);
```

```
console.log("post");
```

Here, our function called done prints out "done". We pass it as a parameter to the setTimeout function, and the second parameter is 1 000 milliseconds, so one second.

What do you think the print-out will be? Try it out for yourself and see!

And while you are at it, what do you think happens if instead of having 1000 as a delay, we use 0?

Experiment for yourself, and try to work out why you think the code behaves like this. In this lesson, we've seen :

- what is a function
- parameters, optional and otherwise
- arrow and function notation
- recursiveness (to calculate the factorial)
- functions used as parameters and callbacks
- the setTimeoutfunction

And as an exercise before we move on to the next lesson, try :

- creating an addfunction that adds two arguments together and returns the answer
- creating a multfunction (bearing in ming that *is the operator for multiplication) and returns the answer
- creating a doOperationfunction that takes three arguments : a function (which could be addor mult) and two numbers, and then sends the corresponding result back

CHAPTER 8

ARRAYS

L et's talk about arrays... Both arrays and object are containers for other things. And they can both be stored in variables.

Arrays are basically an ordered list. There's the first, second, and all the way until the last item. The order in which you put the items inside the array matters.

Objects, on the other hand, are more like dictionaries : you look up a word and the dictionary tells you what the word means.

Arrays and Objects are declared differently : to declare an array, you use square brackets ([...]), whereas to declare an object, you use curly brackets ({...}). And generally speaking, array's should always contain the same type of thing, whereas objects tend to contain a mix:

```
const thisIsAnArray = [1, 10, 15, 200];
```

```
const thisIsAnObject = {
    age: 42,
    type: "Sponge",
    name: "Bob",
};
```

A CLOSER LOOK AT ARRAYS

As we've said before, the order is important in arrays. This means you can add elements on either end, or remove them, and measure the array's length, and so on. Lots of fun stuff that we won't go into just yet.

First, we're going to look at a basic way of looping through an array :

```
let arr = [1, 10, 15, 6, 22, 44];
```

```
for (let i = 0; i < arr.length; i++) {
    console.log(arr[i]);
}
```

Three important things to note here :

- First, we start at 0. In JavaScript, the first element of an array is at the position 0
- Second, an array's length can be read by reading the value of .lengthon the array
- Lastly, to read an element at a given position, we use the []notation. So, the first item in arrat position 0 is arr[0], and the last item is arr[arr.lenth -1].

There are more intelligent ways of doing this. First, we can use for / of:

```
let arr = [1, 10, 15, 6, 22, 44];
```

```
for (let item of arr) {
    console.log(item);
}
```

If you remember, in the last chapter we talked about using functions as parameters in a function.

Well, there's a function that loops over an array, calling the parameter function on every single function in the loop. That function is forEach. So, we can do :

```
arr.forEach((item) => console.log(item));
```

An important thing to note here is that we've created the function that we've passed as a parameter to forEachwithout even naming it. But that's fine, we can do it : it's what is called an anonymous function. (And what other languages would call a lambda function).

Here, the forEachloop just calls the function we've created on each item. Now our function is not doing much, as a matter of fact, we could just pass the console.logfunction :

```
arr.forEach(console.log);
```

A few more functions on the arrays worth mentioning, even though they are outside our scope:

1/.filter(f)will call the function f on every item, and only keep those where freturns a "truthy" value.

So :

```
arr.filter((item) => item > 10);
```

will return:

```
[15, 22, 44];
```

2/ .find(f)will call the function f on every item, and return the first item where freturns a "truthy" value.

Therefore,

```
arr.filter((item) => item > 20);
```

will return 22

POP, PUSH, SHIFT AND UNSHIFT

Just a quick word on 4 useful functions when working with arrays. Thepush and pop functions allow you to add and remove items from the end of an array. More precisely, popremoves an item, and pushallows you to push one or more items on to the end of the array.

```
let names = ["Batman", "Robin"];
console.log(names.pop()); // 'Robin'
console.log(names); // ['Batman']
```

```
  console.log(names.push("Catwoman",    "Alfred"));
// 3 <- the new length of the array
  console.log(names);  // ["Batman",  "Catwoman",
"Alfred"]
```

Conversely, shiftremoves an item from the *start* of the array, and unshiftadds one or more items.

```
  let villains = ["Penguin"];
  console.log(villains.unshift("Joker",  "Bane"));
// 3
  console.log(villains);  //  ["Joker",  "Bane",
"Penguin"]
  console.log(villains.shift()); // "Joker"
  console.log(villains); // ["Bane", "Penguin"]
```

ABOUT EQUALITY AND REFERENCES

Arrays (and functions and objects too) have a somewhat different behaviour, in certain aspects, than numbers or strings or booleans.

If we write

```
let a = [];
let b = [];
```

The aand bvariables might look like they hold the same value, but a == bis false. Why is this? Well, unlike variables that contain numbers, or strings, a and b don't *exactly* contain the array that they've been set to.

You can consider this to be the variables "knowing the address" of where the array is stored.

The code let a= [];creates an array at one address, and let b = [];creates another array at another address. So, when we compare the two addresses, obviously they don't match. (In developper speak, we would say that the arrays are stored "by reference"). Now, this might seem like just a quirk, but it does have important implications. First, let's take a look at this code :

```
let _add = (i) => {
```

```
    i = i + 1;
  }
```

```
let num = 1;
  _add(num);
```

```
console.log(num); // 1 : num is unchanged.
```

Now let's look at this code, which is basically the equivalent for arrays:

```
  let _append = (i) => {
    i.push(1);
  }
```

```
let arr = [];
  _append(arr);
```

```
console.log(arr);
```

What do you think the value of _arris after having run that code?
Try it out and see.

As you can see, the value of arrwas changed (or "mutated" in programer speak). This is because the variables don't contain the array, but the array's address (or reference).

In the _append function, the ivariable is also pointing to the same address. The _arrand ivariables are both pointing to the same address, to the same reference, so any changes that are made on iare also made on arrsince they are the same array.

ARRAY EXERCISE :

6.1 : Given our array, how would you use a loop to sort it so that the values are in order?

```
let arr = [1, 10, 15, 6, 22, 44];
```
6.2. There is a .sortfunction that works on arrays. Look at what happens when we call it with no argument :
```
console.log(arr.sort());
```
6.3.

The sort argument can (and often should) be called with a function argument.

That function takes 2 arguments and returns a number. The way the array is sorted depends on whether the number returned is positive or negative. Try to work out what to write in the sortFunctionbelow to make it sort in the ascending order:
```
let sortFunction = (a,b) => {
// write your code here
}
```

```
console.log(arr.sort(sortFunction));
```
In this lesson, we've seen :

- what an array is (i.e., basically an ordered list)
- how to declare an array,
- three different methods to loop over an array, using two using forand one using forEach.
- We've seen how to add and remove items on each end using push, pop, unshiftand shift
- And we've seen how arrays are actually references.

CHAPTER 9
OBJECTS

L et's talk about objects
As I mentioned in a previous video, both arrays and object are containers for other things. And they can both be stored in variables.

If arrays are basically ordered lists, objects, on the other hand, are more like dictionaries : you look up a word and the dictionary tells you what the word means.

What does that mean for objects?

Well, let's create a dictionary from an object. It's going to be a very limited one because we want to be able to read through it (as humans, I mean) in a few seconds.

For example :

```
let dict = {
   variable: "a box that contains one value",
   boolean: "a type of value that can be true or
false",
   function: "a reusable bit of code",
   array: "basically and ordered list",
   object: "kind of like a dictionnary",
    if: "a keyword that conditionnaly executes
code"
   }
```

Here in this example, the words "variable", "boolean", "array" and so on are called the "keys" of the dict object, and the definitions are called "values".

So, an object is a set of keys and values. And in JavaScript (and in most other languages) the order of the keys does not matter and is **not** guaranteed.

Before we go any further, two points I would like to raise.

First, it is possible to loop over all the keys in an object. So, we can do :

```
for (let key in dict) {
  console.log(key);
}
```

Here, key is logged in turn.

The second point is that to access the values in an array, there are two possible syntaxes that are useful for two different situations.

If I know a key (and the key is just numbers and letters), I can access it directly with the dot notation

```
console.log(dict.function);
```

However, if the key has other characters (like a hyphen), I can access the value using the square brackets notation. I can also use the bracket notation to use a variable to access a value.

So for example, in the loop example above, I can do

```
for (let key in dict) {
  console.log(key, data[key]);
}
```

In the above example, the values were all the same type, but that is by no means a requirement, it's just that we were representing a real-world dictionary.

In most cases, objects will contain values of very different types, and represent the values of one given object.

For example:

```
let user = {
  id: 1,
  name: "David",
  admin: true
}
```

As you can see, declaring an object is fairly straightforward. You can put any kind of value. In my example I've shown a number, a string and a boolean value, but we could also have arrays, and functions, and even other objects.

For example, our object could look something like this :

```
let user = {
  id: 1,
  name: "David",
  admin: true,
  roles: ["Parent", "Educator", "Developper"],
  address : {
    city: "Paris",
    country: "France
  }
}
```

Here we have an array (the roles key) and an object (the address key).

I'd like to touch upon immutability and equality.

Objects behave like arrays when it comes to equality. What do I mean by this? Well, let's take a look at this code:

```
let a = {id: "42"};
let b = {id: "42"};
```

```
console.log(a === b); // false
```

The two objets look the same... But "a" and "b" are references to two different objects, that were created separately, so they are not equal.

Let's try something a little different.

```
let a = {id: "42"};
let b = a;
b.id = 43;
```

```
console.log(a.id); // ...
```

What do you think is logged here?

Well, we've said both "a" and "b" are references. And here, "a" and "b" reference the same object. So, when we change the value of id on "b", we also change it on "a". Because we are referencing the same object. Here the console logs 43.

Now there is another consequence of this. We've mentioned that a and b (and both arrays and objects in general) are references.

Take a look at the following code :

```
const a = {id: 43};
a.id = 44;
```

What do you think happens here? More precisely, we have a const, and we're changing what's happening inside a. So, how do you think JavaScript reacts when we do that?

It likes it just fine.

Why?

Because from JavaScript's perspective, we haven't actually changed "a". Sure, we've changed its contents. But it still "lives at the same address". It still has the same reference. If we do:

```
const a = {id: 43};
const b = a;
a.id = 44;
console.log(a === b);
```

The console log prints out true. It's still the same object. Which means the const keyword is perfectly legal and true. The variable has not varied, even if we've changed its contents.

One last point.

Let's say I have this object and I want to make a copy to manipulate it.

```
const user = {
  id: 1,
  name: "David",
  admin: true,
}
```

If I just do let user2 = user;and then change stuff on user2, the user object will be changed. But let's say I don't want that; I would like to keep the first object safe, and change, say, the id of the new object:

To achieve that, I could do something like this:

```
let user2 = []; // empty array
for(let key in user) {
  user2[key] = user[key];
}
```

```
user2.id = 43;
```
This will copy every single value, then set id to a new value.

However, there is a better, shorter way of doing this.

It's called the ... spread operator.

We can write this :
```
let user2 = {...user, id: 43};
```
This will copy every single key and then set id to 43.

Now, in the case of our user, this will not quite do exactly what I want.

Can you guess why?

The reason is that my user objects contains stuff that are also references. It has a roles array and an address object.

With all the methods above, the user object is copied, but if I change the address it will be changed on both objects.

The same holds true for the roles array.

To really do things cleanly, I need to also "spread" those, for example by doing :
```
let user2 = {
  ...user,
  address: {...user.address},
  roles: [...user.roles]
}
```
As you can see, this can also be done for arrays.

Now, let's talk about another kind of object. The document object model. Or DOM.

CHAPTER 10
THE DOM, BUTTONS, AND BASIC INTERACTIVITY

Hello, in this lesson we are going to take a look at the DOM.

What is the DOM, I hear you ask?

Well, the DOM stands for the Document Object Model, and truth be told most of the time when people talk about the DOM it's just a flash way to talk about what is on the page.

That being said, we do need to talk a little about how an HTML page is built.

Basically, an HTML page is a combination of HTML tags contained within one another.

So for example, we could have a piece of HTML that reads

```
<html>
  <body>
    <div>
      <p>Hello world</p>
      <span>How are you?</span>
    </div>
  </body>
</html>
```

Here we have the <html> tag, that contains the <body> tag, that contains the <div> tag, that contains the <p> and <span> tags, which contains the "Hello" world" text.

Now, the goal here is not to dive deep into HTML structure and styling and so on. But I'm going to try to give you pointers to help you understand how we can manipulate this document.

Now, if you remember in one of the very first lessons, we had a hello world app in the sandbox.

Before we take another look at the JavaScript, of that example, let's take a look at the HTML. If we click on the index.html file on the side, we can see that it is basically:

```
<div id="app"></div>
```

It's elementary. There is basically an empty "div" HTML tag, and it has the id: "app".

Now let's take a look at the
had a bit of code that said :

```
const appDiv = document.getElementById('app');
appDiv.innerHTML = `<h1>${message}</h1>`;
```

Now, in the context, it is fairly easy to read the code : the first line retrieves an HTML element using its id from the document, where the id is "app".

Once it has retrieved the item from the document, it defines a value on it for "innerHTML".

If we look at the display, we can see it has indeed displayed the message. If we inspect the HTML code using the inspector (the one in the Chrome developper tools), you'll see that a h1 tag with our message has been inserted into our div.

Ok, great. What else can we do? Well, we can:

- delete stuff
- read the content of forms
- change attributes on HTML elements
- add interactivity to buttons

Let's start with the last one:

ADDING INTERACTIVITY TO BUTTONS.

What does that mean? Well, basically it is simply defining a function that will be called when the button is called.

Let's open up a Visual Studio Code project, and create a page called index.html

Inside that page, let's write the following:

```
<html>
 <body>
  <button id="btn">Press me</button>
  <script>
  function hello() {
    console.log("hello");
  }
  </script>
 </body>
</html>
```

If we start the debugger (using Chrome this time), a webpage will open up with the button. If we click it, nothing happens.

Now let's add a bit of code to our button, and change it to :

```
<button     onclick="hello()"     id="btn">Press
me</button>
```

Now, if we restart the debugger, we'll see the message appear in the console. Every time we click the button, the hello function is executed.

Now let's make things more exciting.

In the script tag, let's write the following :

```
<script>
  let button = document.getElementById("btn");


  let count = 0;
    function hello() {
      count = count + 1;
      button.innerHTML = "Count : "+count;
    }
</script>
```

Now, when we click the button, the text of the button is updated to show the current count.

Now, we can take this even further. Let's restore the button to its former glory :

```
<button id="btn">Press me</button>
```

Since we have the HTML element at hand, we can set the "onclick" attribute on it directly. So below the hello function we can write :

```
button.onclick = hello;
```

Now that we've talked about triggering functions and writing data, let's talk about reading input from the user.

CHAPTER 11

FORMS, SLIDERS, AND HEX COLOURS

FORMS

O n the web, user input is read via forms.

Now, as I've mentioned before, I'm not going to go into too much depth about how HTML works. The high-level overview is that forms are made up of inputs. The different types of inputs depend on what you actually want from the input. For example, a password input will hide the text, and so on.

Let's try the following :

```
<html>
    <body>
      <form>
        <input id="myValue" type="number">
      </form>
      <button id="btn" >Press me</button>
      <script>
                            let     button     =
document.getElementById("btn");
                            let     input     =
document.getElementById("myValue");
```

```
function hello() {
    window.alert(`you    typed
${input.value}`);
}
button.onclick = hello;
</script>
</body>
</html>
```

Not the most exiting code, but it does… well, what it says it does!

Let's read through it together.

First, the code retrieves the button and the input fields using their ids.

Then it creates a hello function that displays an alert that displays the value of the input field.

When the button is clicked, the code triggers that function.

Now, this could open several possibilities of user interaction. Let's try something a little more complicated.

Instead of the button and form, we're going to create three slider inputs inside a div.

Each slider will look something like this line here:

```
<input    type="range"    min="127"    max="255"
step="1" />
```

And each is in a div so that the inputs at under each other.

Now, let's add an id to each one with the id worth "red", "green", and "blue". The inputs now look something like this:

```
<input    id="red"    type="range"    min="127"
max="255" step="1" />
```

As you might know, on the web (and for computer screens in general) pixels use three primary colours to make all the colours of the rainbow.

These colours are red, green, and blue. And to mix the colours together, we give them different intensities, that are represented as a number between 0 and 255. So pure back is 0 red, 0 green and 0 blue, and pure white is 255 red, 255 green and 255 blue.

The exact mechanics of how that works is not vital, but we're going to use the sliders to change these values and calculate a new colour.

To achieve that, we will create a "colour" object to store all three colour components:

```
const color = {
  red: 127,
  blue: 127,
  green: 127
}
```

Now let's add a div above the sliders

```
<div id="colordiv" style="width: 150px; height:
150px; background-color: #CCCCCC;"></div>
```

Now let's try to set its colour using the colours defined by the sliders.

First, let's create a function to take the red blue and green colours and translate them to a format that our browsers understand.

That format is a hexadecimal (or hex) colour for short. If you've ever seen any CSS code, you've probably come across stuff like the #CCCCCC above, (which is a grey) or #AA99CC (which is a light purple) or #9AFC03 (which is a bright green).

That strange string is actually the three colour components, as base 16 numbers (so counting from 1 to 9 and then A, B, C, D, E, F). In Base 16, or hexadecimal, A is 10, B is 11 and F is 15. And when we have two letters or numbers, we can go from 00 to FF... which is 255 in decimal.

The exact mechanics of this doesn't really matter here, we're just going to take our three numbers and convert them to a hex code.

The conversion of the numbers to base 16 is simple. First, we create a function that takes a number as input:

```
function toHex(val: number) {
  let ret = val.toString(16);
}
```

We need to make sure that we add a 0 in front if there is only one character. We check the length of the variable and add a 0 in from if the length is not 2:

```
if (ret.length == 2) {
  return ret;
}
return "0" + ret;
```

Our full function looks like this :

```
function toHex(val) {
  let ret = val.toString(16);
  if (ret.length == 2) {
    return ret;
  }
  return "0" + ret;
}
```

Now we want to calculate the hex value for the red, green, and blue and set the hex value on the div :

```
function fullUpdate() {
  let red = toHex(color.red)
  let green = toHex(color.green)
  let blue = toHex(color.blue)
  let hexColor = "#" + red + green + blue;
  colordiv.style.backgroundColor = hexColor;
}
```

Finally, we need to get all the sliders, and run a loop on them.

```
for (let slider of sliders) {
  let id = slider.id;
  let update = () => {
    let value = parseInt(slider.value,10);
    color[id] = value;
    fullUpdate();
  }
  slider.onchange = update;
  slider.oninput = update;
}
```

As you can see, for each slider, we read their id.

Then we create an update function for each slider (the update function is written in each loop).

This update function :

- reads the value of the slider and converts it to a number
- then it sets the colour object so that the value corresponding to the id is updated
- lastly, we call the fullUpdate function that sets the colour of the div

Finally, we set this update function to be called whenever anyone uses the sliders.

And "voilà", we have a colour picker!

CHAPTER 12
PROMISES & ASYNC AWAIT

S oon we're going to start using one of the most fun parts of the web. Because the web is not about isolated static pages, it's about communicating and sharing information.

But before we can do so, let's talk about Promises and the async/await notation.

WHAT ARE PROMISES, AND WHAT IS ASYNC / AWAIT?

Well, we want to send a message to the server, and we want it to reply. But that message is going to take a bit of time. Not enough for it to be very noticeable. However, if the JavaScript blocks the page execution, the screen would freeze. And we can't have that. It would produce an awful user experience.

We need to have a way to send a message, and to ask the JavaScript to go and do other stuff.

To achieve that, we define a function a being an asynchronous, using the "async" keyword. So for example:

```
async function update() {
  // do stuff
  return "Hello";
}
```

You'd be forgiven for thinking this function returns a number. As a matter of fact, it returns the promise of a number.

What is a promise?

Let's say I promise I'll tell you a joke, or give you money.

You don't have what I've promised just yet. But you will after a little while.

Now let's transpose this concept to JavaScript. Our code is usually executed immediately. All the instructions of a common block will be executed without the JavaScript engine taking a breath. However, the async notation allows us to tell the javaScript engine that this is asynchronous code. And the await keyword tells JavaScript that it can go and do other stuff while it is waiting for the value to be returned.

A JavaScript promise means something that will be resolved to a value, at some point, but not immediately.

If we log the output of update like this:

```
console.log(update());
```

...we can see that the function does not return hello.

However, we can tell the code to call update, and "then", once the promise is resolved, to call a new function, like this:

```
update().then((value) => console.log(value));
```

If we run this, the console shows "Hello". Now, what do you think happens when we run this?

```
update().then((value) => console.log(value));
console.log("Hi");
```

Try it out and see! Think about why we have this result.

Now that we've had a very brief overview of promises, let's try using them in practice

Let's start by creating our very own Promise :

```
function sleep(ms) {
return new Promise(resolve => setTimeout(re-
solve, ms));
}
```

Don't worry about the "new Promise" syntax for now. It basically means that we are creating a promise. Here, resolve is actually a function (a callback). And we are using setTimeout to say "call the resolve function after ms milliseconds".

So let's try calling that in our update function :

```
async function update() {
await sleep(3000);
console.log("3 seconds gone");
await sleep(1000);
return "Hello";
}
update().then((value) => console.log(value));
console.log("Hi");
```

Now what happens when we run the code? Well, first the console prints out "Hi".

Then 3 seconds go past.

And then another second.

And then the program prints Hello.

Now, it might seem like a detail that the word "Hi" is printed first.

But if you read the code, the update function is called first. So, the sleep(3000)instruction is called first, before the console.log("Hi"). Why is "Hi" executed before the "3 seconds gone" and the "Hello" log?

Well, that is precisely what we mean by asynchronous code. Asynchronous means "not at the same time". JavaScript runs all the synchronous code, then any asynchronous code that is waiting, and then it moves on to other things.

When we wrote:

```
update().then((value) => console.log(value));
console.log("Hi");
```

The line that logs "Hi" is synchronous and runs first. Then the asynchronous code inside update is called.

And this is what allows us to run code that takes time without blocking the user experience. Stuff like … calling web services to retrieve information.

CHAPTER 13
FETCH-ING DATA FROM
AN API

O ne of the means of sharing information is via an API. An API basically means a kind of server that our javascript can talk to directly.

And there are loads of different APIs that can fetch the weather based on where you are, or the number of views on a video, or someone's latest social media posts.

To do so, we will be using a simple JavaScript function called "fetch".

THE FETCH FUNCTION

The way this works is as follows :

We tell the "fetch" function which web address to call. We can also specify what information it needs to send.

Let's start by creating a simple index.html file :

```
<html>
<body>
<h1> Title </h1>
<script src="./code.js"></script>
</script>
</body>
</html>
```

Now, let's create the code.js file mentioned, next to the index.html file, and type in the following:

```
let url = "https://swapi.dev/api/people/1"
```

```
async function update() {
  let data = await fetch(url);
  let ret = await data.json();
  return ret;
}
```

```
update().then((data) => console.log("data", data))
```

As you can see, we are using the async/await notation that we saw when we talked about Promises.

Using fetch is pretty much the same kind of thing as opening a browser to a specific page. Except here it is the code doing the fetching, and the data retrieved is not rendered on screen but parsed in order for the code to retrieve the data it wants.

That is what the fetch does, and it always returns a text file. However, we need to have the code understand what is going on. Thankfully, this API provides data in the JSON format by default, and getting that information from the response is as simple all calling the

Now, if we open the index.html file in Chrome, and open the console, you should see a JSON object printed in the console, which is the data that Chrome has fetched from the server. If you open it up, can you see what the "SW" of swapi means?

ANOTHER EXAMPLE

Now, let's try to have some fun.

Instead of using the SWAPI url, let's try something slightly more complex:

```
let                    title                    =
document.getElementsByTagName("h1")[0];
```

. . .

```
let url = "http://ip-api.com/json";


async function update() {
  let data = await fetch(get_ip);
  let ret = await data.json();
  title.innerHTML = `You are in ${ret.city},
${ret.country}`;
  return ret;
  }


update().then((data)    =>    console.log("data",
data));
```

If we look at the response from the API, we see it is a JSON object, and it has different fields. These correspond to the information the API was able to find out using the IP address we use to call it.

If you go to their website (https://ip-api.com/) you can see for yourself what kind of information is returned.

A FINAL EXAMPLE

Now let's try the following

```
let              title              =
document.getElementsByTagName("h1")[0];


let              url              =
"https://v2.jokeapi.dev/joke/Programming?black-
listFlags=explicit&type=single";


async function update() {
  let data = await fetch(url, {
```

```
method: "GET",
});
let ret = await data.json();
title.innerHTML = ret.joke;
return ret;
}
```

```
update().then((data) => console.log("data", data))
```

Now, what is interesting to note here is that each API returns a different "shape" of data. The SWAPI had one shape. The IP API had another shape —because it was returning a different type of data. And the Jokes API returned yet another type of data. And you can't really tell, with this type of API, what will be returned without actually calling the API, looking at the data and adapting.

Now, obviously we haven't been able to go into everything that's possible with APIs because there are so many. And we haven't even touched on APIs that allow you to write data to the web! But then, that's because each API is specific.

CHAPTER 14
OUR PROJET : A MATH QUIZZ

N
ow is the time to start our project. And we are going to build a math quizz.

Why maths?

Well, we want twenty questions that we can generate in code, and math allows us to do so easily. So, we select an arithmetic operation (for example addition, subtraction, and multiplication). Then we choose two random numbers. Finally, we generate three wrong answers and then ask the player to select the right answer between 4 different choices before the time runs out.

If the time runs out, we move on to the next question. We also need to display a timer.

Simple, right? Well, it might sound a bit complex, but we just need to break the problem down into simple, manageable bits. And I've already prepared the HTML for you to plug in to.

Now, let's get started!

The first thing is to work out how to generate randomness. There is a function for that. Before I explain how to use it, I'd like to show how to fetch that information. In general, when I can't remember the exact syntax for a function, I google MDN, JavaScript and the concept I'm looking for. For example, "MDN JavaScript Random".

This brings up the page for the Math.random() function.

That random will only return a number between 0 and 1, and we want to return an integer. Thankfully, the documentation already has the solution, with the following function:

```
function getRandomInt(max) {
return Math.floor(Math.random() * max);
}
```

So now if we call getRandomInt(5) we get a number between 0 and 4.

Let's create a newQuestion function. And in this function we will start by choosing an operation, and then two numbers.

Let's start by creating a table:

```
const operations = ["add", "sub", "mult"];
```

Now let's store everything in a state object that contains all we need to know the current state of the game:

```
const state = {
questionNumber: 0,
score: 0,
operation: undefined,
a: undefined,
b: undefined,
options: [], // empty array
timer: undefined,
timeLeft: 0
}
```

Now, let's create the newQuestion function

```
function newQuestion() {
// 1. select an operation and set it in the
state
// 2. select the first number and set it in the
state
// 3. select the second number and set it in
the state
// 4. calculate the right answer
// 5. calculate wrong answers and store them in
the options table
// 6. shuffle the table !
// 7. show the question
```

```
  // 8. show the possible answers (in the answer
divs)
  // set remaining time to limit, e.g. 10
  // 10. start the timer



}
```

To select the operation, remember that arrays are indexed with numbers, and their first index is 0. For example, if we have an array called "arr" with say, four numbers, the elements will be indexed with 0, 1, 2 and 3 using the square braquet notation, i.e., arr[0] or arr[3]

Now, we want to select an operation and two numbers, and calculate the result.

Now do you remember our "doOperation" function, back when we were talking about functions? You could use something like that.

Another solution is to write three functions

```
function add (a,b) {
// return the addition of a and b
}


function sub (a,b) {
// return the addition of a and b
}


function mult (a,b) {
// return the addition of a and b
}
```

Then we can write a table with each key that has the same name as a function and as the name of the operation

```
const ops = {
add: {f: add, op: "+"},
sub: {f: sub, op: "-"},
```

```
mult: {f: mult, op: "*"}
}
```

So now if we select a key from the operation array, we can fetch the corresponding function using:

```
ops[key].f
```

For example, if we have two numbers, a and b, we can do:

```
result = ops[key].f(a,b);
```

With that, we can now set the questions.

Now we want to create a "tick" function that updates the timer and checks whether the time has run out

```
function tick() {
// get time from the state
// decrease it by 1 & update the display
// if it is 0, count the question as failed and
start a new question
}
```

Now, when we start a new function, we would like to call this tick function repeatedly. For that, we will use the setInterval function.

```
function newQuestion () {
// 1 through 8
// 9. start the timer
state.timer = setInterval(tick, 1000);
}
```

Now this will work fine the first time, but we also would like to stop the timer if it is already running (when we answer a question and move on to the next one we want the timer to stop).

To achieve that, we want to check that state.timer is set, and then clear the timer before restarting it :

```
if (state.timer) {
clearInterval(state.timer)
}
state.timer = setInterval(tick, 1000);
```

Hopefully, this should be enough to get you started, I've posted the solution with the accompanying code should you get stuck!

BONUS ACTIVITIES :

Update a progress bar to show the time remaining.

Display the current score.

Choose different limits based on the operation (.e.g multiplication is numbers between 2 and 9, for other operations between 1 and 20)

www.ingramcontent.com/pod-product-compliance
Lightning Source LLC
LaVergne TN
LVHW010040070326
832903LV00071B/4474